Anger Management

An Easy To Follow, Step By Step Guide To Anger Management That Will Teach You How To Keep Your Cool Under Pressure And Stay Out Of Difficult Circumstances

(Techniques To Help You Take Control Of Your Emotions And Become A More Loving Parent)

Panayiotis Bekiaris

TABLE OF CONTENT

Developing An Awareness Of One's Emotions And The Current Moment Is Imperative. 1

The Significance Of Thoughts, Perceptions, And Boundaries In Shaping Human Behaviour And Interactions 15

Strategies For Anger Management: Immediate Techniques 46

Assuming Authority Over One's Anger 99

It Is Advised To Refrain From Providing Sustenance To The Habit In Question. 107

Developing An Awareness Of One's Emotions And The Current Moment Is Imperative.

Mindfulness encompasses the practise of residing in the present moment while embracing acceptance, heightened consciousness, tranquilly, and attunement to one's own emotions, thoughts, and sensations, as well as those of others. Furthermore, it involves cultivating an understanding of the surrounding environment and its impact on one's well-being. By cultivating mindfulness or making efforts to develop even a modest level of mindfulness, individuals can effectively address their anger-related challenges.

Chronic anger can arise from various stimuli, including but not limited to a lack of acceptance, harbouring grudges, inadequate emotional self-awareness, the tendency to pass judgement and assign negative labels to one's own emotions and those of others, dwelling on past events, preoccupying oneself with future concerns, and neglecting to cultivate a compassionate approach towards one's anger. By practising mindfulness, individuals can experience various advantages, including the following:

Individuals possess the ability to identify the specific stimuli that elicit anger inside themselves and acquire effective strategies to regulate such emotional responses. This entails adopting a mindset that avoids assigning excessive significance to these triggers and instead recognising them for their inherent nature.

One acquires the ability to embrace the present moment and derive satisfaction from its inherent qualities, free from concerns regarding past events or future uncertainties.

Individuals tend to exhibit increased involvement in the immediate work at hand, thereby mitigating the tendency to recollect negative experiences that evoke feelings of frustration and wrath.

Individuals tend to exhibit a greater level of engagement and productivity in their assigned duties when they cultivate a genuine interest and derive enjoyment from them.

One acquires the capacity to sense one's feelings in their unadulterated state, without excessively interpreting or analysing them.

The individual demonstrates a willingness to acknowledge and embrace their own emotions, as well as the emotions of others, without resorting to categorising them as inherently negative or undesirable.

One acquires the ability to embrace circumstances as they unfold and to readily release and dismiss negative encounters.

As one begins to observe these advantages, the task of managing one's irascible disposition or subdued hostility becomes more feasible. One comprehends the concept of deriving pleasure from the current moment, maximising its potential, and utilising each instance to cultivate a life of contentment.

In order to achieve this objective, it is recommended to initiate the implementation of the following measures:

When undertaking a work, it is important to approach it with mindfulness. It is imperative to maintain a heightened level of mindfulness and attentiveness throughout each individual action, demonstrating a genuine curiosity and investment in the outcomes and advantages that may be derived from those actions. Enhancing one's engagement in a task, deriving enjoyment from it, and improving performance are facilitated by maintaining a heightened awareness of one's emotional state. This heightened awareness enables individuals to promptly recognise instances of anger or the emergence of anger-related emotions, thereby facilitating the redirection of attention back to the ongoing task when one's thoughts begin to wander. Mindfulness additionally fosters the development of cognitive attentiveness towards one's triggers, enabling individuals to effectively manage and resolve them subsequent to the completion of their ongoing work. In the event of experiencing intense rage, it is advisable to discontinue the current task and address the emotional state of anger.

When one becomes aware of the emergence of rage within oneself, it is advisable to accept its presence rather than dismissing it, and direct one's attention towards it. One should refrain from categorising or characterising it as inherently negative or unfavourable; rather, one should acknowledge it as an emotional state that seeks to convey insights or messages pertaining to one's personal identity or circumstances. Pay attention to the message that the emotion of rage is attempting to convey. Perhaps the intention of the message is to convey insights pertaining to an individual's worries, apprehensions, guilt, or other related psychological phenomena.

In the interim, it is advisable to refrain from responding to the aforementioned stimulus. One can effectively manage impulsive behaviour by engaging in a state of calmness and adopting a mindful approach of observing one's anger without immediate action. Continuously observe the situation and allow it to diminish naturally.

The initial 5 to 10 minutes may present challenges, particularly due to the ingrained habit of responding to feelings of rage. After the initial challenging moments have elapsed, one's wrath will gradually diminish. Engaging in this practise whenever experiencing anger might yield surprising results in terms of rapid emotional soothing, enhanced self-regulation, and the cultivation of more self-discipline.

As one cultivates a sense of acceptance towards their own anger, it is advisable to extend this practise to encompass others as well. In the event that an individual expresses anger towards oneself, whether it be a friend or a spouse, it is advisable to refrain from passing judgement or harbouring negative perceptions about this individual. Alternatively, it is advisable to allow them sufficient time to comprehend and process their feelings of anger without immediately responding to its outward manifestation. If it is possible for you to maintain silence, please do so. If not, it is advisable to remove yourself from the situation temporarily.

While the individual in question has not yet reached the same level of recognition and treatment of their anger, you possess the ability to assist them in this regard. Engage in a conversation with the individual once they have regained a state of calmness, and endeavour to assist them in cultivating a heightened awareness of their emotions while refraining from assigning evaluative labels to these emotions.

By implementing these three strategies, individuals may experience a reduction in anxiety and stress levels, as well as an improvement in emotional regulation. By developing an understanding of one's own emotions as well as the emotions of others, and refraining from reacting impulsively to instances of anger displayed by individuals in one's vicinity, there will be a notable enhancement in one's emotional intelligence.

Mindfulness meditation is a contemplative practise that involves directing one's attention to the present moment with an attitude of non-judgment

Mindfulness meditation, despite its historical presence in diverse religious traditions spanning over two millennia, did not gain significant traction in the Western world until the 1970s. This shift in reception can be attributed to the emergence of several studies that provided empirical evidence of tangible health advantages associated with this practise. These benefits extend beyond the enhancement of mental well-being to encompass improvements in physical well-being as well.

Consequently, this phenomenon sparked a resurgence in the adoption of mindfulness and a fresh comprehension of its multifaceted benefits in enhancing one's well-being, since it directly addresses the underlying factors associated with anxiety-induced health concerns. Mindfulness meditation, supported by empirical research, has gained significant traction throughout various governmental establishments in the United States, encompassing correctional facilities and healthcare institutions.

Engaging in mindfulness practises facilitates a heightened comprehension of one's ideas as distinct entities from one's actions, concurrently fostering mental tranquilly. These cognitive and emotional benefits are particularly salient while endeavouring to enhance anger management strategies. Initially, it is advisable to engage in the cultivation of mindfulness inside a controlled setting, wherein one can be certain of an absence of external disruptions. However, over time, individuals can progress to a stage where they are capable of practising mindfulness in a wide array of contexts, irrespective of temporal or spatial constraints. Mindfulness can be regarded as a viable option for individuals seeking a means of diverting their attention away from the present circumstances, so allowing sufficient time for the dissipation of anger.

To initiate the process, it is advisable to locate a suitable environment that offers comfort and tranquilly, allowing for a duration of around 10 to 15 minutes of uninterrupted sitting. To commence, it is advisable to engage in a series of deep, deliberate inhalations and exhalations. During this process, it is essential to take into account the sensory aspects associated with the inhalation and exhalation of air, including the tactile sensation, auditory perception, and gustatory experiences. Subsequently, it is imperative to broaden this level of consciousness to embrace the remaining faculties of perception. The human body consistently offers a vast array of sensory information, which can be accessed by individuals who are receptive to it. By cultivating openness to these sensations, one can experience a greater influx of sensory information than anticipated.

Ultimately, the objective should be to attain a mental state characterised by a state of minimal cognitive activity. In the immediate timeframe, however, directing attention towards sensory stimuli might effectively serve as a mechanism to attenuate the continuous flow of thoughts that are, in all likelihood, persistently present within one's mind. Mindfulness, when employed in real-time, can be beneficial in managing anger-related concerns by facilitating a temporary disengagement from the source of anger, so enabling individuals to regain emotional composure. To obtain further information

The Significance Of Thoughts, Perceptions, And Boundaries In Shaping Human Behaviour And Interactions

Given the subject matter of human emotions, it is important to acknowledge that objectivity is not universally applicable and that the topic is characterised by shades of grey rather than absolutes. The presence of ample space for ambiguity, subjectivity, and irrationality is evident. Anger, similar to other emotions, is influenced by individual cognitive processes, interpretations, and personal limits. Individuals possess unique characteristics, resulting in diverse manifestations of rage within each person.

The factors that elicit a strong emotional response from me may not have the same effect on you, perhaps leaving you unaffected. Similarly, what I perceive as a minor inconvenience can be deemed intolerable and provoke intense frustration in your case. Hence, the measurement of rage is inherently challenging due to its subjective nature, as it is contingent upon individual perception. The text undergoes filtration using our distinct methodology.

However, even after considering that aspect, there are still certain phenomena that are universally recognised as sources of anger, while others are deemed insignificant and not worth the effort. One may potentially face allegations of overreacting if they were to exhibit hostility in response to an incident such as the unauthorised removal of their sandwich from the communal refrigerator in a workplace setting. In the broader context, this matter holds relatively little significance and is generally not seen as highly important.

Nevertheless, the significance of this matter may be of great importance to you due to undisclosed external circumstances. For instance, consider a scenario where one individual possesses highly stringent dietary specifications that were adequately fulfilled by the aforementioned sandwich, a feat never accomplished by alternative food options. Alternatively, one may experience feelings of anger due to the perceived absence of respect or concern exhibited by others towards one's efforts and personal belongings.

The pivotal significance of personal boundaries

Essentially, individuals' anger triggers or thresholds are determined by their individual boundaries. What is the maximum amount you are willing to accept? From whom does the information originate? What is the duration of the specified time period? All of these factors are crucial in the endeavour to create one's limits and determine the threshold at which they are violated. Which domains exhibit a high degree of stringency, wherein tolerance for mistakes or delays is minimal? Perhaps you possess a diminished capacity to tolerate individuals that engage in deceitful behaviour, although you appear to exhibit a somewhat higher level of resilience towards derogatory remarks. Alternatively, one may hold the view that dishonesty is permissible, while simultaneously expressing an inability to tolerate others who fail to uphold their commitments.

The range of examples is extensive due to the individual variations in perceived limits across social, emotional, and physical domains. This phenomenon is observed in those who have a high propensity for physical contact, juxtaposed with those who maintain a significant distance from engaging in tactile interactions with others. Invading an individual's personal space without obtaining prior consent may potentially elicit a strong emotional response characterised by intense wrath. The unpredictability of anger triggers necessitates a cautious approach towards our verbal expressions and actions in order to maintain interpersonal harmony. Demonstrating respect towards people and their personal boundaries is a hallmark of civilised behaviour, serving as a proactive measure to mitigate potential conflicts.

Cognitive processes and subjective interpretations have the potential to either incite or mitigate feelings of rage.

It is vital to bear in mind that anger may not always be warranted. While certain individuals may purposefully engage in behaviours aimed at inciting a reaction or triggering emotional responses, many others may inadvertently cause distress without being cognizant of their actions. In the majority of instances, their actions were negligible; it is the perception of the observer that attributes significance to their actions. I would want to provide an explanation. In those who already experience anxiety and exhibit a propensity for anger, or are consistently subjected to stress, pressure, and feelings of being overwhelmed, maintaining a clear perspective can prove challenging. This particular atmosphere induces a sense of distrust and a slight inclination towards paranoia.

As a result, individuals may find themselves consistently susceptible to being triggered by even the most trivial occurrences, regardless of their harmless nature. One illustrative instance that might be provided is the scenario wherein an individual perceives that another person is discussing or making reference to their own self. I possess a considerable breadth of experience in this domain as a result of personal encounters in the past. I possessed a notable degree of personal insecurity and was confronted with a considerable amount of social anxiety, the existence of which I was previously oblivious to. I consistently had a heightened state of vigilance due to the pervasive belief that individuals were consistently engaging in derogatory discourse, disparaging remarks, or clandestine conversations about my person.

On multiple occasions, I experienced anger in response to a perceived offence, only to subsequently recognise that the comment made by an individual was not intended to be derogatory towards me. In reality, frequently it was not primarily centred about my person. However, I was firmly entrenched in my pervasive belief that everyone harboured ill intentions against me, resulting in a distorted perception of the world that deviated significantly from objective truth. Individual introspection, personal uncertainties, and heightened self-consciousness contribute to a heightened susceptibility to unproductive and incorrect expressions of anger. It required a significant amount of time for me to come to the realisation that my anger was not directed towards these individuals, but rather towards myself.

Conversely, I am acquainted with an individual who exemplifies a positive outlook on life, consistently maintaining an upbeat demeanour and perceiving the proverbial glass as half full. The individual in question possesses a remarkable ability to perceive the world and its inhabitants without discerning any faults or malevolence, thereby leading to a scarcity of instances where she experiences anger. What is the rationale behind this request? Due to her lack of justification and perceptual limitations, she remains oblivious to evident reasons that are apparent to others. The individual's pervasive optimism engenders a sense of trust in others and a propensity to perceive their positive qualities. However, this inclination can be disadvantageous when individuals attempt to use her. Conversely, it also guarantees that she does not experience unwarranted anger.

Transient Affective States

As previously said, rage can be classified as a secondary emotion that arises as a consequence of main emotions, such as fear or grief. Individuals who experience persistent anger may potentially exhibit symptoms of depression, anxiety, or a comorbidity of both conditions. Depression and anxiety are not merely transient emotional states seen in our daily lives. These mental diseases have the potential to shape our lifestyles in a distinct manner compared to individuals with sound mental health in our immediate environment.

Anger is often regarded as a transient emotional state that arises due to underlying psychological disorders. The intense emotional experience of rage may be perceived as a contributing factor to the development of depression and anxiety. It is important to conduct a more comprehensive analysis in order to ascertain the underlying factors that have precipitated the initial manifestation of rage. Various factors can potentially elicit the manifestation of this particular feeling, although it should be noted that these factors do not constitute the primary underlying cause.

Upon experiencing anger, individuals may encounter difficulties in promptly identifying the fundamental origins of fear and anxiety that could have triggered their rage. One may also direct attention towards the one who appears to have elicited the emotional response. Consider a motorist exhibiting aggressive behaviour on the road, commonly referred to as road rage, and contemplate a scenario where another driving abruptly enters their lane. The driver may attribute their negative emotional state and potential receipt of a speeding penalty to the presence of the other vehicle they are driving around. Subsequently, the individuals in question will proceed to assign culpability to the driver for their tardiness, while also attributing any other perceived faults to said individual. It is conceivable for individuals to assert that it serves as the underlying factor for their experience of anger; nonetheless, this assertion lacks veracity.

If a different driver had been present instead of the individual exhibiting road rage, it is possible that they would have been indifferent to the situation. Individuals may exhibit a friendly gesture, such as smiling and waving, towards another driver who has cut in front of them, as they possess an empathetic comprehension of the anxiety and difficulties associated with driving and traffic conditions. The absence of causality can be attributed to the fact that various individuals would have responded to the driver's behaviour in diverse manners. The driver's road rage was not caused by the one who cut them off. However, it was the underlying factors that contributed to the development of rage as a more instinctive response to a perceived danger.

When attempting to ascertain the origins of one's anger, it is crucial to examine the specific facet of one's life that is being jeopardised. Is there someone causing harm to your reputation? Does a someone exist who consistently undermines your self-worth or diminishes your sense of value? In order to facilitate the resolution of potentially contentious situations, it is advantageous to identify and acknowledge the specific elements that are being deprived from us.

Human beings have an inherent inclination to safeguard and uphold their reputation, frequently making concerted efforts to shield their public perception. Naturally, individuals prioritise ensuring their well-being through the acquisition of essential resources such as sustenance, housing, and financial stability, so enabling them to maintain functional survival. Regrettably, our reliance on pride is also a factor. The preservation of one's dignity is motivated by the desire to communicate one's inherent value and entitlement to recognition and inclusion within society.

The experience of feeling belittled, embarrassed, ashamed, or any other form of negative emotion has the potential to induce anxiety in individuals. The inclination to validate oneself in the eyes of others is a manifestation of collective psychology. Human survival often relies on interdependence with others. The potential loss of that particular form of assistance has the potential to elicit feelings of fear inside us.

When an individual perceives a potential threat or attack to their self-image, it often triggers a defensive response aimed at safeguarding and preserving that image. Consequently, certain individuals experience significant distress when subjected to ridicule by others. While it is acknowledged that inappropriate jokes exist, it is important to recognise that even seemingly harmless teasing can provoke genuine negative reactions in certain individuals.

The study revealed a correlation between heightened anger and subsequent sexualization of women. The objective of the study was to determine the potential reactions of men when their masculinity is perceived to be under danger. The concept posited that males would experience a compulsion to assert their dominance over females, employing the promotion of specific beliefs centred around control as a means to achieve this objective. In situations where a male perceives a potential challenge to his masculinity from a woman who possesses greater intelligence, he may engage in efforts aimed at asserting dominance. According to Dahl et al. (2015),

The implications of the research suggest that when a woman rejects a man, it has the potential to elevate levels of rage in men. Evidently, there exists much heterogeneity among males; nonetheless, within our societal context, a significant number of men are socialised to exhibit a pronounced sense of pride. Certain individuals may exhibit a preoccupation with continually affirming their masculinity as a means of safeguarding their perceived social standing. Individuals may be reluctant to appear ashamed or perceive themselves as inferior to the idealised version of masculinity they hold. This study has demonstrated that male individuals exhibit anger when faced with women who exceed them in a given test, and may potentially engage in sexual objectification of women as a coping mechanism to alleviate their feelings of inferiority.

This observation indicates that the individuals in question has a vested interest in safeguarding their reputation on a global scale. Individuals must take measures to safeguard their personal profiles in order to authenticate the information they possess regarding their own identities. When individuals' ideological beliefs are challenged, they may respond defensively in order to safeguard their beliefs, leading to expressions of anger and hostility (Pratt, 2014).

Approach situations with a relaxed and nonchalant attitude.

It is imperative to approach certain circumstances with a lighthearted perspective and seek amusement even in the gravest of situations. In essence, laughter serves as an inherent physiological mechanism that safeguards the body from potentially detrimental emotional states, such as melancholy and rage. Nevertheless, it is imperative to take into account two factors when implementing this approach:

Acquire the skills necessary to refrain from dismissing the issue and resorting to a nonchalant response of laughter. It is imperative to confront and resolve problems, as well as address any sources of anger or frustration by communicating them to the responsible party. Failure to do so may perpetuate the unpleasant behaviour. The function of laughter is to facilitate the process of approaching a challenging problem with a lighter perspective, so enhancing one's ability and inclination to effectively address and resolve it.

It is advisable to avoid employing sarcastic humour or excessively serious attitudes towards others, as sarcasm is considered an undesirable expression of rage that does not contribute to problem-solving. Furthermore, it is important to refrain from becoming easily offended by snarky remarks. The individuals in question may be highlighting your areas of vulnerability through the use of humour. However, it is important to perceive these remarks as jests while simultaneously making efforts to address and rectify the specific behaviour or flaw that the other party is bringing to your attention. In addition to experiencing amusement, individuals possess the capacity to modify their previously unfavourable conduct.

It is advisable to actively participate in behaviours that are more productive and beneficial.

Rather than resorting to physical acts of aggression, such as striking a wall or mistreating a pet, individuals experiencing anger might explore alternative activities to effectively channel and redirect the energy associated with their emotional state. A variety of activities can be pursued, such as physical exercise or participation in sports, involvement in artistic endeavours, or even the act of reading literature.

Understanding effective strategies for managing anger can significantly reduce the likelihood of engaging in aggressive behaviours and enhance emotional self-regulation.

In a devout manner, seek forgiveness through prayer.

It is advisable to engage in prayer and seek divine intervention to facilitate the process of forgiving individuals who have caused harm and against whom one harbours feelings of wrath. According to the biblical passage in Colossians 3:13, individuals are encouraged to exhibit gentleness and a willingness to forgive, while refraining from harbouring resentments or grudges. According to The Living Bible translation, it is emphasised that individuals should have in mind the act of forgiveness demonstrated by the Lord, so compelling them to extend forgiveness towards others.

Maintaining resentment against an individual who has caused harm prevents one from establishing a harmonious connection with the divine. It is advisable not to delay the process of forgiveness until one has the inclination to do so, as it is likely that such inclination may never arise. In contrast, it is advisable to make the conscious decision to extend forgiveness, irrespective of one's emotional state. By placing trust in a higher power, such as God, to aid in the process of forgiving, it is likely that one's emotional disposition will undergo transformation throughout this journey.

In order to effectively re-channel your energy, it is recommended to engage in a contemplative and reflective practise, such as prayer, which allows for a focused and intentional redirection of one's internal resources.

Rather of expending one's energy on feelings of pain, hatred, and revenge, it is advisable to seek divine assistance in channelling this energy towards constructive and beneficial endeavours. The divine entity will present opportunities for individuals to engage in small actions that have the potential to enhance their own personal growth as well as positively impact those in their immediate vicinity.

7. Develop a strategic approach for addressing future instances of provocation.

As long as humanity exists within the global context, instances of transgressions and instigations will persist. Nevertheless, it is imperative that we do not allow ourselves to be governed by these adverse emotions. Those of us who adhere to the principles of divine obedience are occasionally required to confront and surmount these assaults through the application of God's love. It is advisable to mentally prepare oneself by strategizing appropriate verbal and behavioural responses when faced with challenging individuals or tense circumstances that have the potential to elicit rage. Subsequently, upon encountering these circumstances, one will possess a structured course of action to adhere to.

The act of surrendering to God is a fundamental aspect of religious devotion and spiritual practise.

Do you experience frustration or disappointment due to the lack of fulfilment of your prayers? Alternatively, do you harbour resentment towards the negative experiences you have encountered throughout your life?

Many individuals share this sentiment. A considerable number of individuals have experienced feelings of anger towards a divine entity at various points in their lives. The optimal approach to address this matter entails engaging in sincere communication with the divine being and expressing one's thoughts and concerns. When individuals approach the divine entity with sincerity and humility, expressing their discontent over the occurrences that have transpired in their lives, they will experience a profound sense of divine love enveloping them, accompanied by the enlightenment imparted by the divine Spirit, leading to the acquisition of previously unknown knowledge.

In his literary work titled "Surviving in an Angry World: Finding Your Way to

Personal Peace," Charles F. Stanley, a renowned author and pastor, advises individuals who harbour resentment towards God due to circumstances permitted by Him to candidly acknowledge their anger, but subsequently release it promptly following its expression.

If individuals fail to promptly confront their feelings of hatred towards God, it is likely that the devil will exacerbate the corruption of their spirit by introducing more profound malevolence. It is imperative that individuals demonstrate a willingness to entrust their faith in God unconditionally, as He possesses an unwavering love for humanity, possesses comprehensive knowledge on the optimal path for one's existence, and exclusively permits circumstances that foster personal growth and fortitude.

On the twelfth day of the intervention, participants are encouraged to engage in the practise of cognitive restructuring.

The subsequent phase entails initiating a cognitive shift. It is worth noting that individuals may have an increased propensity for engaging in profanity, insulting others, displaying theatrical reactions, employing hyperbole, or demonstrating irrational behaviour when experiencing anger.

In the event of a single mishap, do you tend to exhibit a cognitive bias wherein you automatically extrapolate that all subsequent events would invariably result in negative outcomes? However, it is important to acknowledge that regardless of personal emotions, the situation does not constitute a literal global catastrophe. One may engage in self-dialogue by expressing the following sentiment: "The current situation is indeed exasperating, yet it is comprehensible." Expressing anger in the present moment will not lead to a resolution of the issue at hand.

Furthermore, this does not signify the ultimate catastrophe.

It is advisable to refrain from employing terms such as "always," "never," and "forever" in academic discourse. It is advisable to refrain from using profanity or employing language that carries a negative connotation. Instead, it is recommended to consciously substitute such phrases with positive or neutral alternatives. It is advisable to exercise caution and refrain from uttering statements that have the potential to create a sense of exclusion, embarrassment, or offence towards the individual with whom one is engaged in conversation. The emotion of anger has consistently shown ineffective in resolving problems, instead serving as a hindrance to the timely identification and implementation of solutions.

Employ logical reasoning to facilitate personal growth and problem-solving. It is a universally acknowledged fact that individuals encounter unfavourable circumstances or periods of misfortune at various points in their lives. It is imperative to bear in mind that the cosmos does not harbour any animosity towards individuals, nor does it possess a deliberate intention to inflict misery upon them. Consider this perspective: the universe is preoccupied with matters of greater significance than causing disruptions in your life.

Furthermore, it is important to acknowledge that one should not use their wrath to impose expectations upon others. The desire for equitable treatment, recognition, and consensus is a universal aspiration among individuals. However, it should be noted that these factors do not provide absolute assurances. The aforementioned entities are not obligated to you. All of these entities originate from the concept of respect, which necessitates the acquisition of merit. The reciprocation of regard is a prerequisite for asserting one's entitlement to respect. The coexistence of anger with respect is not possible.

When encountering a persistent furious idea, it is advisable to allocate sufficient time to subject it to scrutiny and evaluation. This approach provides an effective means of contemplating a subject matter and arriving at a definitive resolution. For instance, if an individual experiences anger as a result of excessive work-related stress impeding their ability to take breaks, this scenario lends itself to empirical investigation. The procedure involves engaging in typical behaviour for one week, assessing one's overall efficacy, subsequently incorporating additional breaks during the next week, evaluating one's overall efficacy once again, and subsequently comparing the two assessments. This approach shifts the entire process from a theoretical standpoint to a practical one, enabling empirical testing and yielding tangible outcomes that can be reliably utilised.

If encountering a cognitive impasse lacking a readily verifiable resolution, it may prove beneficial to instead engage in an examination of the existing body of information and ascertain the potential insights that may be derived from such an endeavour. In order to accomplish this task, it is vital to engage in a comprehensive analysis of the given circumstance, followed by documenting one's cognitive processes that determine the perceived state of affairs. Additionally, it is essential to identify and document all evidence that substantiates the notion that one's perception of the situation may be distorted. In the event of recent job loss and a prevailing sense of persecution, it is worth acknowledging the elevated unemployment rate within one's locality, which has engendered a shared predicament experienced by numerous individuals. When confronted directly with evidence, one is likely to encounter greater difficulty in evading the truth compared to when negative thoughts are present in one's mind without proper contextualization.

Strategies For Anger Management: Immediate Techniques

Offering guidance to individuals on how to effectively manage their anger, maintain a state of calmness, or adopt a relaxed demeanour may appear straightforward in theory. However, implementing these strategies in practise often proves to be somewhat challenging. This book aims to provide readers with effective strategies for managing anger, rather than simply offering hollow advice. It will present legitimate and empirically supported techniques to assist individuals in gaining control over their anger.

When one experiences a quick onset of anger, rationality tends to be disregarded, leaving only uncontrolled fury as the predominant emotion. This is not an opportune moment to engage in a rational analysis or problem-solving endeavour. Such activities should be postponed until one has successfully achieved a state of emotional equilibrium, allowing for the manifestation of sensible behaviour, rather than exhibiting characteristics reminiscent of the fictional character known as the Incredible Hulk.

This chapter presents a selection of reliable strategies that can be employed as immediate measures to effectively manage rage.

The first tip pertains to the historical countdown.

Indeed, the time-honored strategy of utilising a countdown mechanism has proven to be efficacious, persisting as a prominent method for inducing tranquilly amid instances of anger, frustration, or restlessness.

In instances where one experiences anger, is in the process of becoming furious, or anticipates being angry, it is recommended to promptly close one's eyes, engage in deep breathing, and initiate a counting exercise. The countdown sequence from ten to zero was observed. Was the attempt unsuccessful? In order to further explore the subject matter, it is advised to inhale deeply and repeat the aforementioned action, with the option of doing so repeatedly if desired. Alternatively, one may choose to commence with the numerical value of 50 in the event of experiencing intense feelings of anger. The countdown sequence from 50 to 0 is observed.

Even if an individual experiences a state of calmness prior to reaching the numerical value of zero, it is advisable to persist and complete the countdown. One has the option to engage in mental counting or employ the usage of fingers as a cognitive diversion. Regardless of the approach chosen, this technique consistently yields positive results for individuals across the board.

Tip #2: Techniques for Respiratory Exercises

An alternative to numerical enumeration is the utilisation of breathing exercises, commonly employed in the practise of Yoga. In instances of heightened rage, it is advisable to pause and assume a seated position. If feasible, place your arms on the chair and proceed to shut your eyes. Inhale deeply, briefly retaining the breath; subsequently, exhale slowly and deliberately. Reiterate the method: inhale, pause, exhale. Inhale, pause, exhale. In order to maintain consistency, it is recommended to replicate the identical pattern for a minimum duration of five minutes, encompassing around 15 to 20 iterations.

The subsequent phase entails the challenging task of redirecting one's focus away from extraneous thoughts and directing it towards the act of regulating one's breath. Disregard one's current location and ongoing activities; disregard any ambient noise, such as a vociferous employer or a clamorous youngster. The sole emphasis is placed on the act of respiration. In order to enhance concentration, individuals may employ techniques such as regulating their breathing patterns or engaging in counting exercises, which serve to divert their attention and maintain cognitive engagement.

Following a brief duration, individuals may experience a reduction in anger and a subsequent state of bodily relaxation.

Third Tip: Alter Your Focus

In circumstances wherein an individual finds themselves positioned within an extended queue, experiencing impatience due to the presence of a couple engaged in a vociferous altercation directly ahead, a crying infant situated in close proximity behind, and the anticipation of a few additional minutes of waiting, it is not uncommon for feelings of anger to arise. What actions should one take in the event of abruptly becoming a victim of a similar circumstance? One must redirect their attention, naturally.

In order to mitigate the impact of a seemingly insurmountable predicament, divert your attention towards a distant object for a duration of around two minutes. Various objects can be observed, such as a potted flower situated at a distance, a movie poster, the buttons located within an elevator, or a floral print adorning an individual's clothes. Direct your gaze on the thing and engage in a thorough observation - meticulously perceive the various hues, endeavour to envision or recollect the tactile qualities; focus your attention entirely on the object.

Redirect your attention after a duration of one minute, and if you have more available time, direct your gaze towards an alternative subject. Here it is. There is a limited opportunity to experience anger, regardless of the level of frustration one may have felt in the preceding moment.

When the situation exceeds acceptable limits

There exist varying degrees of emotional distress. Anger, in essence, is an intensified emotional state that lacks regulation. Given our innate tendency to experience dissatisfaction with specific circumstances, it becomes imperative to establish clear boundaries and effectively terminate such discontent. In order to determine the appropriate cessation point, it is advisable to assess the intensity of one's anger on a scale ranging from 1 to 10. The initial annoyance level, denoted as 1, is a common level of irritation that may be experienced. This level has the potential to intensify incrementally until reaching 10, which signifies the highest degree of aggravation. At this point, one's emotional state may become significantly compromised, resulting in a complete loss of composure. One approach to assessing one's current emotional state is to engage in a comparative analysis with previous experiences.

If an individual perceives their rage level to be at or above a rating of 6, it might be inferred that they are entering a zone of heightened risk. Upon reaching that juncture, it is probable that one might observe any of the subsequent phenomena:

One may experience a desire to designate the object of their fury as their adversary or cultivate a sense of animosity towards the target of their rage.

The sensation being referred to can be characterised as engaging in a conflictual encounter with another individual.

One desires to vocally express their discontent directly towards another individual.

Despite being aware of the inappropriate nature of such actions and having no intention of carrying them out, individuals may have a subjective inclination towards violence or physical aggression as a perceived suitable response in some situations. This inclination may manifest as a want to physically harm someone, such as by hitting them, or to engage in destructive behaviour, such as overturning furniture.

The user's text does not contain any information. The human body experiences a sensation of tightness or tension. One's hands may exhibit clenching behaviour, while the act of grinding one's teeth may also be observed. The sensation pertains to the need for exerting bodily restraint upon oneself.

The aforementioned descriptions share a similar characteristic, namely, the manifestation of highly intensified negative emotions. This entails the gradual escalation of one's level of aggravation from a relatively low intensity of 2 or 3 to a significantly heightened level of 10.

At that juncture, the expression of fury transitions into a detrimental and deleterious state. Individuals may experience a tendency to respond impulsively without thoughtful consideration, leading to a perception of being unapproachable by others in their social circle, whether or not they are cognizant of this behavioural pattern.

The primary objective is to minimise the occurrence of negative emotions. Furthermore, individuals are likely to avoid finding themselves in a situation where they utter the phrase, "Oops!" Upon reflection, it appears that I have beyond reasonable limits in my actions. In light of the irreversible consequences that have ensued, it is evident that the most effective approach to managing one's anger is through proactive measures aimed at prevention.

The concept of "unapproachable aggression" refers to a behavioural pattern characterised by a tendency to exhibit hostile and confrontational behaviour that

Many individuals may choose to conceal their anger, as they struggle to manage their emotions. This phenomenon is sometimes referred to as latent aggressiveness. This phenomenon occurs when individuals engage in activities such as procrastination, pouting, and uncertainty, while simultaneously pretending that everything is going well. Dormant hostility arises from a desire for self-sufficiency. It is highly probable that assistance may be desired in handling the task. Examine in advance with regard to the concept of 'vehement indignation'.

The concept of open aggression refers to the overt display of hostile behaviour or violent actions towards others. It is characterised by a lack of

On the other side, a significant number of individuals have resorted to aggression and anger as a means of expressing their emotions, often resulting in physical or verbal aggression that can cause harm to themselves or others. This phenomenon is occasionally referred to as Open Aggression. This narrative and analysis encompass several elements such as conflict, irritation, restriction, criticism, vocal outbursts, arguments, and comedic elements. The manifestation of open aggression originates from an inherent need for self-sufficiency. This is evident in the culmination of conclusive anger.

The robust propensity to elicit awe can be effectively managed and rationalised through the processes of communication, normalisation, and supportive assistance in adapting to various circumstances. This assertive vexation can contribute to the development of relationships. The suggestion is to engage in premeditated thought before to verbal expression, exhibiting excellence in articulation while being mindful of the context in which it is conveyed, while also remaining receptive and adaptable to alternative perspectives. This implies displaying restraint, refraining from raising one's voice, expressing oneself only while experiencing internal satisfaction, and genuinely attempting to comprehend the emotions of others. While you impress awe with confidence, you demonstrate that you are genuinely and conscientiously committed to your institutions and yourself.

The several classifications within the field of psychology.

Three different types of wonder regions were observed by advisors using a specific methodology.

The phenomenon of rapid and profound astonishment

The phenomenon of swift movement and profound admiration is commonly associated with the imperative for insurance coverage. It is a phenomenon that is observed in both humans and a variety of other animals, and it occurs when the animal experiences pain or distress. This particular manifestation of difficulty exhibits a tendency to wander without a clear direction or purpose.

An Examination of the Various Classifications of Anger

The following are some classifications of anger:

The concept of repressed rage refers to the psychological phenomenon in which individuals consciously or unconsciously suppress or inhibit their feelings of wrath.

The suppression of emotions leads to the suppression of anger. Repression occurs when individuals choose to disregard and avoid direct acknowledgment of their emotions. It is possible to hold the belief that by disregarding them, they will ultimately resolve themselves without external intervention. When individuals engage in prolonged suppression of their sensations and emotions, these internal experiences tend to gain more prominence. This frequently results in heightened anger and outbursts of aggressive conduct. The prolonged consequences of this particular manifestation of anger can have detrimental impacts on both our physical and psychological well-being.

The concept of righteous wrath refers to a morally justified emotional response to perceived wrongdoing or injustice.

This form of fury frequently correlates with individuals' political and religious convictions. This form of rage is deemed unacceptable because to its potential for escalation and the subsequent risk of violence.

Passive-aggressive fury refers to a form of expressing hostility or frustration indirectly, rather than openly and directly. It involves the use

This phenomenon refers to a form of anger expression characterised by the redirection of frustration and fury onto a target or object that is not the primary source of the emotional distress. We continue to hide our anger, but it arises in inappropriate times and even against people who are closest to us. We don't admit our anger or create boundaries. Instead, we start mistreating other people, which makes them feel horrible about themselves. We may start becoming cold to someone or ignore them totally.

Rage

Anger and anger are identical in origin but distinct in degree. Anger becomes significantly more harmful when coupled by wrath. However, whether fury grows relies on how we use and handle our anger.

Rage is the highest level of wrath, and it's often shown physically. It causes adrenaline and other chemicals associated with rage to spike.

The Difference Between Anger and Rage

Anger, in itself, isn't related with shouting and violence. Anger gives us a sense that we need to take care of ourselves. It makes us more aware of our surroundings, and it minimises our chances of being manipulated. It supplies us with protection and assurance. If we discriminate between these two, we realise that anger alone isn't enough to result in physical violence.

Rage is different from anger since it's a highly destructive emotion that may make any scenario potentially life-threatening. Anger can remain within our conscious control; anger, however, isn't under our control.

The failure to deal with anger healthily can cause us to feel additional stress. As we know, our emotions are interlinked, so when we can't figure out what we're experiencing, this might lead to wrath, which means we end up "exploding" on someone or something.

Rage isn't simply subject to the effect of external factors; it can also develop from our inner surroundings. When this happens, it's harmful to our personality, leading to self-sabotaging and sentiments of hatred for oneself. This inward, bottled-up wrath can also manifest externally.

Some people who've experienced wrath claim it causes them to become an entirely different person—someone who's lost complete control over themselves.

Reflexology/Acupressure

Massaging or pressing certain trigger spots in your body can relieve pain, decrease anxiety/depression and ease anger. In the case of anger, the middle finger is involved. All you have to do is to massage or press the length of the middle finger of your right hand for 3 to 5 minutes. Switch to your left hand and do the same. While doing these, inhale and exhale deeply. Continue the action until your anger has subsided. Refer to the image in chapter 13 for the other pressure points.

Sound therapy

Natural sounds can be calming and therapeutic. All you have to do is to listen to the sounds of nature and they would appease you. Lie or sit down comfortably in a place where you won't be disturbed. Listen to the sounds of the falling rain, the blowing wind, the wooing sound of the waves, the chirping of birds, the waterfalls, and similar sounds of nature. Some people prefer soft music of their favorite songs. It doesn't matter what sound you choose, provided that it calms you.

The phenomenon of hypnosis

The utilization of hypnosis, administered by a licensed professional, has been shown to be effective in assisting individuals in the management of anger, anxiety, and stress. However, it is not advisable for individuals with psychiatric conditions. It has the potential to exacerbate their illness. Additionally, it is imperative to verify the credentials and legitimacy of the individual doing the operation.

Auto-suggestion, also known as self-suggestion or self-hypnosis, refers to

In this approach, individuals engage in the repetitive self-suggestion of desired good behaviors with the aim of acquisition. The process might be likened to self-hypnosis, wherein concepts are deeply ingrained into the subconscious mind, resulting in subsequent alterations in behavior. It is recommended that this task be performed on a daily basis. It is also possible to perform this action multiple times within a single day.

The professional roles of psychologists and psychiatrists are significant in the field of mental health.

This represents the final recourse when all other options have proven ineffective. It is advisable to get assistance from a qualified professional who possesses the necessary licensure, as they can provide guidance in effectively regulating emotions such as anger, stress, and worry. The psychologist will provide guidance in identifying positive behaviors and understanding their benefits in comparison to harmful actions.

EXERCISE: RAPID RESPIRATORY ATTENTION

The purpose of this exercise is to facilitate the observation of the fundamental mechanics of one's breath. The act of breathing serves as a valuable tool for monitoring our present state and facilitating a connection to bodily consciousness. Prior to gaining insight into our internal state, it is important to cultivate an awareness of our breath. As previously said in the preceding chapter, the act of immersing oneself in the present moment is a crucial aspect of effectively managing one's anger. Individuals have the ability to engage in introspection by focusing on their breath, enabling them to assess their well-being and observe their body's reactions to prevailing circumstances. The cultivation of mindfulness towards the breath enables individuals to actively engage with their body, so providing a means to alleviate tension and anger.

There is no requirement to assume a comfortable posture or engage in the act of lighting a candle in this context. This activity can be performed in any location and at any time. Locate a specific area adjacent to or within the nasal passages. If experiencing nasal congestion, consider employing an alternative method involving the oral cavity. Maintain a high level of concentration on that particular location. Inhale deeply and observe the characteristics of the breath. Exhale the breath in a same manner. While engaging in the act of respiration, it is necessary to observe and discern several attributes. Is the length of my breath short or long? The inquiry at hand pertains to the depth or shallowness of a particular subject matter. Is the air perceived as cool or warm? Can the experience be categorized as good, unpleasant, or neutral? Does the sensation appear to be localized within the thoracic region or does it extend deeper into the abdominal cavity? Please assess all the aforementioned facets of respiration, and if you perceive the ability to decelerate or intensify your breath, feel free to engage in such modulation.

The Impact of Anger on the Human Body and Brain

Anger can be understood as a physiological reaction within the human body. The phenomenon of fight or flight can be conceptualized as an intricate interplay between two distinct regions of the human brain that are primarily responsible for ensuring personal safety and promoting survival. The brain region that exhibits the highest reactivity and primitiveness, which is conserved across species including reptiles, demonstrates a heightened responsiveness to various forms of stimulus. The human body responds to a stimuli by activating the fight or flight response, leading to a subsequent reaction.

The paleomammalian brain exhibits a higher level of sophistication, incorporating emotions as a more advanced mechanism for responding. These systems are specifically engineered to facilitate the release of cortisol, adrenaline, and various other hormones, so enabling the individual to actively participate in combat. When subjected to a significant level of activation, the cerebral region responsible for housing certain cognitive faculties exclusive to the human species undergoes a literal state of cessation. In certain regions, blood circulation may cease. This phenomenon is commonly observed among individuals who report a lack of recollection regarding events that occurred during episodes of anger, or an inability to comprehend the motives behind their own actions. In numerous instances, there exists a biological basis for such assertions.

Hence, the significance of this study cannot be overstated.

The user's text is already academic in nature. No rewriting is necessary. The concept of body scan refers to a technique used in various fields, such as medicine, psychology, and mindfulness practices. It involves

In the preceding exercise, an examination was conducted on the phenomenon of respiration. An alternative approach involves extending this heightened state of consciousness to encompass the entirety of the physical form. This exercise is a well recognized practice used in various ancient and contemporary traditions. Its purpose is to cultivate a heightened sense of bodily awareness by directing attention to the ongoing sensations and processes occurring inside the entirety of the body.

This exercise can be performed in various postures, including standing, seated, or lying down. The objective of this exercise is to conduct a comprehensive scan of our body, with the aim of identifying and acknowledging feelings experienced over the entire range, from the crown of the head to the soles of the feet. Begin by assuming the selected position. Engage in a brief period of mindful breathing, directing your attention to your physical sensations and allowing each breath to be taken as fully as possible within your current capacity. Please proceed to direct your attention on your scalp. Attempt to accurately focus on this specific region of your anatomy. If one finds this task challenging, it is important to acknowledge that it is part of a larger process. Take a minute to observe any difficulties encountered during the exercise without passing judgment. Examine the contents of the scalp. Maintain focus on this particular area for a brief duration, subsequently transitioning towards the temples. It is important to emphasize and concentrate on the subject matter with great precision. Subsequently, we shall proceed in a descending manner. As we systematically observe the facial features, namely the cheeks, eyes, nose, mouth, and chin, what observations can be made? Does the individual experience any sensation of pain? Is there any evidence of clenching? Alternatively, may it be posited that we are already in a state of relaxation? Does the sensation of tingling occur? Do the sensations that we perceive elicit feelings of pleasure, displeasure, or neutrality?

We proceed to examine the remaining sections of our physique, attentively observing and investigating each component. The anatomical regions of interest encompass the neck and throat, the shoulders, the arms and hands, the chest and upper back, the stomach and lower back, the pelvis and the seat, the legs, and ultimately, the feet. After completing the task, it is advisable to assess the state of your breath and determine whether its characteristics have undergone any alterations. If an individual perceives a heightened state of relaxation compared to their initial state, they may engage in a broad scanning process to identify any lingering sensations of discomfort or tension. Subsequently, they can direct the calm energy they have attained towards the specific area experiencing stress. This provides individuals with the chance to not only enhance their mindfulness through the practice of body scanning, but also to promptly utilize its advantages in order to foster a deeper engagement in the management of their anger and stress.

The drawbacks associated with rage significantly outweigh its benefits, and its prevalence continues to increase at an alarming pace.

> The fundamental question at hand is to how we, as a society, effectively address and resolve the issue of rage.

Do anger courses and anger management programs effectively address the issue at hand?

The response to the question is dual, encompassing both an affirmative and negative aspect.

In order to provide a comprehensive overview of the discourse, it is important to evaluate two contrasting perspectives, or assumptions, pertaining to the subject of rage.

Do persons who experience intense rage genuinely possess the motivation to address and resolve their anger issues permanently?

Does enrolling in anger management courses imply a long-term commitment?

A considerable number of individuals who experience anger fail to recognize their own emotional state as anger.

During childhood, individuals acquire knowledge about anger through their environment and parental figures. They see the behaviors of others and internalize the significance of anger as both a functional mechanism and a tool. During childhood, there is a lack of encouragement to effectively express anger, as we are taught that it is unacceptable to feel intense anger. Additionally, we often face reprimands when we have a legitimate reason to experience anger. In the realm of emotional expression, the phenomenon of uncommunicated fury manifests as a form of soundless and intangible anger.

Over a period of time, and by deliberate repetition, rage undergoes a transformative process, resulting in a dynamic and regrettable sequence of events.

The majority of the human population is not born with a predisposition towards anger. Certain individuals have discovered the means to employ rage as a mechanism for survival - an adaptive strategy to overcome challenging situations. The repetitive use of the tool transforms into a behavioral pattern. Regrettably, this behavior is not appropriate for the majority of situations in everyday life.

Anger management programs mandated by the court

It is commonly portrayed in the media that a significant portion of anger management courses are marketed to cater to court-mandated anger management requirements. In contrast to the broad evaluation conducted via online examinations, it is evident that the utilization of court-ordered rage courses and workshops represents just a small proportion of the overall help provided.

Each individual harbors a sense of intense anger towards a certain matter and consistently possesses the entitlement to experience such emotions. Effectively managing anger is a skill that requires a high level of education, just as acquiring the ability to value and respect fury is a scholarly expertise.

Achieving long-term resolution of anger extends beyond the mere consumption of instructional manuals, seeing videos on anger management techniques, and engaging in positive thinking. The everlasting arrangement involves the modification and reconfiguration of fundamental behavioral patterns, as well as the release of pent-up fury that is suppressed within the body and psyche of the individual experiencing anger.

The process of effectively managing anger in a lasting manner involves identifying and addressing the underlying emotional charge associated with a particular memory or situation that elicits a behavioral response. This process is not purely cognitive, but it does require a conscious decision to initiate the process.

Anger management classes serve a crucial purpose as an initial step in acquiring knowledge about new strategies and healthy approaches to resolving anger. Anger courses and seminars provide a method for initiating the process of healing. Similar to any newly acquired skill, developing proficiency in managing anger in a healthy and proactive manner requires practice and a strong desire to improve.

The presence of others obstructs your path. The cashier's pace of service is notably sluggish, characterized by an excessive amount of verbal communication, which consequently prompts a desire to promptly conclude the transaction and depart. Upon entering your vehicle, it becomes apparent to you that a significant number of individuals in the parking lot are exhibiting suboptimal driving behaviors. The commute back to one's residence may not exhibit any improvement. The individual expresses their frustration by audibly signaling their displeasure through the use of a vehicle horn, physically gesturing with raised hands, and vocalizing offensive language towards any motorist who obstructs their path. The dissipation of wrath and irritation is contingent upon the engagement in a home-based activity that serves as a distraction.

In the present scenario, an apparently inconsequential incident elicited an intense emotional reaction. Such types of outbursts may not necessarily be considered a typical or expected response. It is important to clarify that rage does not exclusively encompass the range of intense emotions that individuals can experience. Individuals have the capacity to experience emotions at a heightened level above what is considered typical. If you identify that in yourself, you may be looking for strategies to manage or cope with your extreme emotional responses.

Tips for Managing Emotions

The subsequent techniques might be employed to facilitate the regulation of one's emotions. Certain aspects may appear evident, but others may possess a more nuanced nature. The purpose of these suggestions is to establish a basis for developing self-awareness of one's emotions and effectively managing them.

Avoid expressing your initial thoughts without careful consideration.

In situations characterized by heightened emotional intensity, individuals often express statements that they subsequently experience remorse or regret for having articulated. In instances of heightened emotional states, individuals may be more prone to engaging in deliberate acts of insult as a means of self-protection. Although the immediate gratification may be satisfying, it is probable that there may be negative consequences in the future. Making an inappropriate statement at an inopportune moment has the potential to detrimentally impact a relationship. Instead, it is advisable to allocate sufficient time to formulate a response that is grounded in logical reasoning. Counting to ten before responding can be a beneficial strategy for certain individuals.

Engage in a conversation with a confidant to discuss and explore your emotional experiences.

Attempting to resolve the problem independently can prove to be exceedingly challenging. Having a strong support system consisting of close friends and family members can provide valuable assistance and encouragement throughout one's personal journey. Indeed, it is a veritable axiom that the involvement of numerous individuals in a given task or endeavor significantly reduces the burden and effort required to accomplish it. Relying on one's support system can yield unexpected levels of assistance. Additionally, it alleviates certain responsibilities from one's shoulders. The individual remains accountable for regulating emotional intensity; nevertheless, engaging in verbal communication significantly aids in this process.

Assessing Your Stress Level.

Individuals who frequently encounter heightened emotional states often do so in the context of experiencing substantial levels of stress. Conduct a self-evaluation to determine whether an excessive level of stress is present in your life. Take into account the various obligations arising from your professional responsibilities, educational pursuits, familial and social relationships, as well as the personal standards you set for yourself. The mitigation of stress levels has been found to play a significant role in the regulation of emotional reactions.

Engage in a temporary disengagement from one's problems.

Taking a pause when necessary is deemed acceptable. Adopting a real-time approach to managing an emotional issue may not align with your individual needs and preferences. Engaging in a process of disengagement, emotional regulation, and deliberate problem-solving can provide significant efficacy. The inclusion of a time constraint has the potential to augment stress levels, thereby heightening the magnitude of one's emotional reaction.

Attempting to gain perspective from another individual's standpoint is a valuable exercise.

During a condition of heightened emotional arousal, individuals tend to have a cognitive bias towards self-focused attention, primarily directing their thoughts towards their own emotional experiences. Engaging in perspective-taking for a little while can contribute to one's emotional regulation. Recognizing the validity of one's emotions might contribute to grounding oneself.

Be vigilant for indications that may precede an event or situation.

Gain an understanding of the physiological and psychological processes that occur within the mind and body as they prepare for heightened emotional states. The ability to regulate one's emotions can be achieved by exerting cognitive control when one becomes aware of warning signs or indicators. It is imperative to adopt a rational mindset and maintain composure in order to effectively manage the situation without succumbing to emotional outbursts. Engaging in self-dialogue during the meeting can help maintain a state of calmness and rationality.

The initial two groups, namely the indifferent and the neutral, are referred to as the observers. The importance of their presence in our lives is often underestimated. The observers act as a backdrop for individuals and may maybe provide help to those in need. This analysis will facilitate the development of awareness and foster a state of mindfulness and appreciation when encountering these individuals. It is imperative to uphold a demeanor that is characterized by grace, authenticity, and politeness when interacting with individuals. This will be beneficial for both parties involved, while also contributing to the establishment and enhancement of your professional standing. Individuals who consider themselves as being of lower social status are likely to exhibit heightened awareness and gratitude towards individuals who demonstrate mindfulness and politeness towards them. It is imperative to exhibit consistent and affable conduct towards individuals, irrespective of one's relative position of influence or prestige within their particular milieu.

The manner in which we engage with the final two categories, namely the positive and negative groups, differs due to the presence of connections rather than mere exchanges. Every interpersonal connection necessitates a certain degree of trust, respect, and the establishment of boundaries.

The positive aspects

In order to foster pleasant and uplifting connections, it is imperative to maintain a state of mindfulness. What is the rationale behind this? Due to our emotional attachment, it is common for us to hold elevated expectations regarding their reciprocation of our feelings. In the event that the other party fails to reply in the anticipated manner, it is possible that we may find ourselves in a state of desolation, leading us to infer that we have incurred their dissatisfaction. Feelings of anger and resentment may ensue as a result. In this context, it is imperative to refrain from voluntarily relinquishing our authority to the aforementioned individuals. Maintaining our authority and self-worth while simultaneously demonstrating respect for others is an essential imperative. Developing proficiency in this skill necessitates consistent effort, although once attained, it can foster the emergence of profoundly exquisite, peaceful, and mutually respectful long-term partnerships.

It is noteworthy that individuals, supported by our admiration, have the tendency to project their positive attributes onto others, leading to a significant increase in emotions of respect towards them. In this particular instance, it is imperative to engage in introspection and contemplate the aspects that elicit admiration towards these individuals. It is important to acknowledge that the qualities one admires in others often reflect aspects of oneself, as the recognition of such traits would not be possible without their presence inside oneself. By maintaining a state of mindfulness and awareness, individuals have the potential to flourish and beyond their own expectations.

The phenomenon of aggressive anger is a subject of academic inquiry.

Aggressive rage might be considered as the antithesis of passive anger. Individuals that exhibit violent rage consistently possess a heightened level of emotional self-awareness, yet often lacking insight into the underlying causes of their anger. The manifestation of aggressive rage often leads to acts of violence, as individuals experiencing this emotional state frequently struggle to pinpoint the underlying causes of their anger. Consequently, they tend to divert their outbursts towards themselves, those in their immediate vicinity, or even inanimate things. The proposition that aggressive rage is not superior to passive anger is supported by the argument that it compels individuals to engage in impulsive and irrational behavior. Individuals that exhibit aggressive anger tendencies typically display a proclivity for being furious in response to a wide range of stimuli, even seemingly inconsequential matters. Moreover, their expressions of anger often manifest in an explosive or retaliatory manner. The consequences include physical harm to both property and individuals. Indicators of aggressive anger encompass manifestations such as engaging in road rage, perpetrating domestic violence, vocalizing loudly or shrieking, engaging in destructive behavior as a means of expressing anger, participating in physical altercations, exhibiting prolonged outbursts of anger, issuing threats to others, and similar behaviors.

There exist many variations of anger.

Chronic rage refers to a persistent and unmanageable form of anger that typically manifests as frequent and intense episodes of outbursts and fits. This particular manifestation of rage has the potential to impact the functioning of the immune system and give rise to various forms of psychological problems.

Guilt-induced fury typically arises from the experience of guilt, regardless of its validity or lack thereof. Typically, self-directedness is the primary focus rather than being directed towards others. An illustration of rage resulting from guilt can be observed in a scenario when an individual unintentionally becomes the cause of another person's demise. This phenomenon might potentially induce feelings of guilt, subsequently transforming into wrath that is focused inward against the individual.

Overwhelming anger typically arises from an individual's limited capacity to effectively manage the excessive pressures and challenges presented by life or the specific situations they encounter. Individuals may encounter circumstances that prove to be overpowering, leading to difficulties in effectively managing them. Consequently, they may choose rage as a coping mechanism to conceal their underlying problems. The cathartic outcome of this fury typically manifests in self-inflicted harm or harm against individuals or items in their vicinity.

Individuals that exhibit judgmental rage typically do not possess an inherent disposition towards anger, but rather, their anger arises as a consequence of harboring resentment towards others. This type of fury arises from adverse emotional states, including but not limited to envy, jealousy, and perceptions of unfairness. For example, an individual may develop feelings of resentment towards another individual whom they perceive as superior to themselves. At its onset, the sensation may appear innocuous, resembling a mere sentiment of displeasure. However, as it intensifies, it evolves into an all-consuming rage, rendering its containment or cessation arduous. If not curbed, judgmental anger most times serves as a motivating force for grievous acts such as assault, rape, or even murder.

There exist numerous categories of recognized anger issues, and it is evident that these anger disorders exhibit common physical, emotional, and psychological indicators that facilitate their identification.

Assuming Authority Over One's Anger

Acknowledging one's challenges is commonly regarded as the initial phase in achieving personal growth and attaining a sense of empowerment. It is imperative to exercise restraint over one's anger, as doing so can yield significant positive transformations in one's life. However, the task at hand is not devoid of challenges and, in reality, it might prove to be equally arduous as the endeavor to overcome substance dependency. Although individuals may not experience severe withdrawal symptoms, they will consistently confront a formidable adversary in the form of their own self.

It is imperative to avoid underestimating the significance of anger management difficulties and to refrain from assuming that one's problems can be swiftly resolved. The process of breaking the anger pattern and retraining cognitive and behavioral responses to various situations necessitates a substantial investment of time, effort, and self-discipline. After making the decision to address one's anger issue, there are several measures that can be taken to regain control.

Identifying the Underlying Source

Occasionally, an individual's expression of rage may appear to be spontaneous and inexplicable to its observers; nonetheless, it is seldom devoid of any underlying cause or motivation. The expression of anger, even in response to trivial matters or little transgressions committed by individuals, can be traced back to underlying causes. It is plausible that the individual's loss of composure may not be directly correlated with the present circumstances. The potential cause may be attributed to the individual's daily experiences and the accumulation of pressure and/or stress. The manifestation of such behavior may stem from unresolved emotional issues, a background of abuse, or substance misuse. After acknowledging the presence of an anger issue, the subsequent phase involves exploring the underlying causes that contribute to the difficulty in effectively controlling anger. Numerous self-help strategies and advice exist that enumerate a range of symptoms potentially associated with rage. However, it is crucial to recognize that self-help advice should serve solely as preliminary signs that may need seeking professional assistance. The accurate diagnosis of a mental health condition can only be accomplished by an individual who has received specialized training in the field.

Assess the efficacy of the proposed solution.

After selecting a solution that aligns with your perceived competence, the next step involves evaluating its effectiveness through practical implementation and observation. As previously said, an individual's level of awareness of the impact of their actions and reactions on others directly correlates with their total personal development and effectiveness.

Seek Assistance—And Expand Your Perspective

When individuals embark on the initial stages of adopting a novel problem-solving approach, it might be advantageous to collaborate with a reliable confidant, a close relative, or a professional counselor. In our individual spheres, it is common practice to seek counsel from acquaintances when confronted with complex predicaments, prior to making any consequential decisions. It is recommended to incorporate practice exercise 6 into your weekly routine by selecting one or two problems to work on. By consistently engaging in this practice, the six-step process will gradually become more ingrained and effortless for you. The six-step strategy defined in this chapter has shown to be one of the most pragmatic approaches for anger management. This approach can be applied to a diverse array of challenges and across a broad spectrum of scenarios. The crucial aspect lies in fostering an open mindset and granting oneself the capacity to approach one's predicaments from alternative perspectives. Through practice and experience, individuals can enhance their ability to develop solutions that are not only effective in the short term but also have long-term efficacy.

The main points of discussion are as follows:

The manner in which individuals address societal problems establishes the foundation for potential improvements, deteriorations, or the maintenance of existing situations in their lives.

Negative social problem solving is typified by hasty decision-making, reactive behaviors driven by anger, evasive behavior, and a reliance on the expectation that issues would resolve spontaneously.

Positive social issue solving is distinguished by a cheerful, patient, and meticulous approach towards addressing challenges, wherein problems are perceived as opportunities to be confronted.

The application of the six-step approach to problem-solving in social contexts is versatile and can facilitate the identification and implementation of constructive resolutions for the challenges encountered.

The process of social problem solving involves a series of steps. Firstly, it is crucial to clearly identify the problem at hand and generate potential solutions. This entails outlining the problem in specific and tangible terms, which is accomplished in steps 1 and 2. Secondly, it is necessary to assess the likely outcomes associated with each potential solution. This involves considering both short-term and long-term consequences, which are evaluated in steps 3 and 4. Thirdly, the most optimal solution is selected from the menu of options and implemented. This entails choosing the most suitable course of action from the available alternatives, as outlined in step

5. Lastly, the effectiveness of the chosen solution is evaluated. This involves reflecting upon the decision-making process and utilizing the experience gained to further develop one's problem-solving skills, as indicated in step 6.

It Is Advised To Refrain From Providing Sustenance To The Habit In Question.

Similar to other emotions, anger has the potential to be nurtured or intensified. The experience of rage is perpetuated by continued exposure to circumstances that elicit frequent and intense emotional responses.

Once the factors that elicit anger have been identified, individuals must make a choice between either continuing to disregard the situation or actively seeking resolution.

Indulging in the inclination towards anger may manifest as a response to a provocation, with the awareness that one's reaction would be highly intense.

Another possibility is the assumption of additional responsibilities or employment opportunities, despite the potential inability to effectively manage them.

Engaging in behaviors that contribute to the heightened prevalence of anger in one's life. It is a common occurrence for individuals to be associated with those who elicit feelings of fury or hatred.

The concept of "feeding the habit" pertains to the deliberate engagement in anger-provoking circumstances with the intention of eliciting a response.

Your participation in self-defeating behaviors is evident.

Various factors such as the use of alcohol, drug usage, the presence of certain things, the actions of specific individuals, or the engagement in particular habits have the potential to serve as triggers for anger within one's personal experience.

In order to properly manage and address anger, it is imperative for individuals to refrain from engaging in behaviors that contribute to its manifestation.

Jumping to conclusions

They are a prevalent source of rage stimulation in both domestic and professional environments. In summary, the act of concluding entails making assumptions on individuals' emotional states and their intentions to cause distress, without affording them an opportunity to clarify their perspectives and intentions.

In the context of a romantic partnership, it is possible to encounter a situation when one's male partner engages in covert telephone conversations without disclosing the nature or participants of those interactions. Nevertheless, the term 'secret' that you allude to could potentially lead one to suspect that their romantic partner is engaged in an extramarital relationship. This assertion may deviate significantly from the veracity. The primary rationale lies in the observation that individuals engage in concurrent phone conversations, speak in hushed tones, and withhold information, which does not necessarily imply infidelity. Instead of hastily making assumptions and inciting anger, it is advisable to approach her in a composed manner and inquire about the nature of those phone calls, providing an opportunity to elucidate one's own perspective.

Inconsequential annoyances

This phenomenon pertains to the tendency of individuals to accumulate minor disappointments and irritations over an extended period, leading them to actively seek out potential sources of distress. This phenomenon mostly impacts marital relationships. Instead than allowing flaws and problems to accumulate until they reach a critical point, it is advisable to address them promptly.

Regardless of its magnitude, it is imperative not to disregard any problem that arises, as doing so might have a significant impact on one's life. It is imperative to proactively address any factors that may potentially jeopardize a relationship, since allowing such elements to accumulate over time might lead to a point of irreparable damage. To effectively manage one's responsibilities and remain proactive, it is essential to address difficulties using multiple strategies. By employing several approaches, individuals may ensure they stay well-informed and in control of their tasks consistently.

The concept of guilt displacement

In situations where outcomes deviate from initial expectations, individuals often find it convenient to assign blame to external parties. A considerable number of individuals encounter challenges in identifying flaws, regardless of the circumstances. This phenomenon frequently engenders feelings of rage and discord among acquaintances, relatives, and coworkers.

Instead of consistently criticizing others, it is imperative for each individual to assume accountability for their own conduct. This ultimately facilitates the management of the repercussions of anger, thereby addressing unwarranted fury that is not attributable to any individual.

What are the physiological indicators of anger?

In order to enhance our ability to manage anger, it is necessary to acquire the skill of identifying and acknowledging the presence of anger inside ourselves. Numerous individuals afflicted with anger management problems perceive their emotions in a dichotomous manner, characterized by a binary perspective. The potential emotional responses of individuals in this scenario encompass a range from intense anger to a state of tranquility. In actuality, rage does not adhere to a binary framework, but rather manifests as a nuanced and multifaceted emotional state. Violence can manifest along a spectrum that spans from intense rage to a state of relative tranquility, with individuals typically experiencing their anger at varying degrees between these two extremes.

Individuals who derive satisfaction from witnessing heightened levels of fury will inevitably face numerous challenges when confronted with the need to recognize and accept their own experiences of intense rage. Nevertheless, irrespective of immediate recognition, individuals will invariably encounter behavioral, emotional, and physical indicators that can be employed to communicate the onset of anger.

Let us examine several distinct indicators that individuals may observe in relation to the emotion of rage. This aids in introspection and facilitates the identification of one's personal passion, enabling individuals to assess the urgency of addressing it.

As a result, in conjunction with the process of socially constructing a certain reality, there exists a simultaneous production of deviant or problematic realities, commonly referred to as the social construction of social problems. Certainly, it is imperative to acknowledge that every departure from the norm does not inherently constitute a societal issue. In accordance with

Spector and Kitsuse (2001), it may be argued that regardless of whether one examines the construction of deviance or the perception of deviation as a social problem, the underlying process remains comparable. This is due to the absence of any objective definition or categorization of deviance or social problems. As previously mentioned, the building of a social problem, much like the development of a given reality, is influenced by both individual and collective subjectivities. The perception of reality as a social issue is contingent upon its social construction, as posited by Spector and Kitsuse (2001). According to Merton and Nisbet (1971), the classification of a particular action or phenomenon as a social problem necessitates its recognition as a transgression of established social standards, alongside the perception of a substantial portion of individuals who view it as a breach of the collective moral conscience. The statement aligns with the perspective put forward by Berger and Luckmann (1986) regarding knowledge as a corpus of veracity, specifically referring to the established principles of behavior that guide humans, commonly known as social norms. According to Merton and Nisbet (1971), the aforementioned phenomenon can be seen as a dialectical interplay between the collective moral consciousness and the apparent presence of social issues. In this context, the collective moral conscience plays a role in objectifying certain realities as social problems. Likewise, the perception of social problems serves to reinforce the collective moral consciousness. Therefore, when social groups label a certain action or situation as a social problem, they are essentially expressing a value or moral judgment.

This description serves as the foundation for the imperative to take action in order to maintain this collective awareness. The concept of collective morality has been discussed by Merton and Nisbet in 1971. This process of defining social problems is therefore based on the value attributed to certain actions and/or on the resulting interests (Spector and Kitsuse, 2001), the institutionalization of which makes it possible to overcome them.

Similarly, Spector and Kistuse (2001) and Loriol (2012) put forth the concepts of "claim-making activities" and "claim-making process" as mechanisms for the formation of social problems. The phenomenon consists of three primary phases that coincide with the constructivist viewpoint of the entirety of existence. The process involves the identification or creation of a problem by a collective of individuals, typically experts, who possess a vested interest in the matter. Subsequently, efforts are made to raise awareness of this problem among the general public through various methods, including awareness campaigns, media dissemination, conferences, and so forth. Finally, the problem enters a stage of institutionalization, wherein it is officially recognized and defined, and measures are established to address it, thereby granting it legitimacy. In relation to the initial phase of discovery or invention of an issue, as previously mentioned, it is important to note that a social problem does not possess an inherent objective existence, but rather emerges through a collaborative process of definition. Social problems arise when a collective of individuals assess specific circumstances and, by their subjective evaluation, identify a necessity to address, enhance, or modify them (Spector and Kitsuse, 2001). In order to accomplish this objective, these collectives of individuals will endeavor to garner awareness towards the societal issue they perceive as unacceptable or in conflict with their moral principles, and strive to rally a wide array of individuals and organizations to endorse their advocacy. This particular phase is commonly referred to as the "enterprise of morality." Not every collective of persons will possess the capacity to progress their assertion. Undoubtedly, the successful execution of such an endeavor necessitates a specific locus of authority, such as that held by politicians, governmental bodies, specialists, media entities, and the like. Additionally, it demands a commitment to safeguarding and promoting entrenched interests, as well as a comprehensive understanding of the subject matter at hand. Frequently, these collectives consist of individuals who perceive themselves as authorities in a particular domain due to their specialization, hence establishing the guidelines and norms to be adhered to. These collectives of individuals employ several strategies, including protests, lobbying, media engagement, and conferences, among other methods, as well as employing techniques that objectify their subjective experiences and manifest them in the broader social sphere. The phenomenon that will thereafter be absorbed by those who are part of the same social sphere. Therefore, this process generates a novel conceptualization of a social issue that is acknowledged by the entirety of society and can now serve as a point of reference for individuals. In order for the revised concept of the social problem to become an inherent component of social reality, it necessitates institutionalization. The social problem is defined and objectified within official papers, so conferring upon it a fixed and legitimate character. The provided definition of the institutionalized social problem serves as a framework that individuals can utilize to ascribe significance to a particular reality. Additionally, it serves as the foundation around which various actions are formulated to address the social problem (Loriol, 2012).

One of the challenges individuals may have is the struggle to maintain focus and concentration.

There are various behavioral manifestations that may serve as indicators of attention-related challenges in children, which are commonly associated with Attention-Deficit/Hyperactivity Disorder (ADHD). The following are instances of individuals who are of school-age:

The individual exhibits a lack of capacity to maintain focus on a singular task, as well as experiencing challenges in successfully finishing tasks before to succumbing to feelings of boredom.

The challenge of auditory perception due to external disturbances

One of the challenges that individuals may encounter is the difficulty in adhering to given directions and effectively comprehending and assimilating information.

It is important to acknowledge, nonetheless, that these behaviors are frequently observed in young children.

The act of fidgeting and squirming

The illness originally known as attention deficit disorder (ADD) is now commonly referred to as attention deficit hyperactivity disorder (ADHD) within the medical profession. This change in terminology is due to the recognition that ADHD often encompasses not just attention deficits but also hyperactivity and impulsivity. This phenomenon is particularly evident among youngsters in the preschool age group.

Indicators of hyperactivity that may engender the presumption of attention-deficit/hyperactivity disorder (ADHD) in young children encompass excessive restlessness and agitation.

Individuals exhibiting hyperactive behavior may experience difficulty remaining seated during activities that require a quiet demeanor, such as mealtime or listening to someone read aloud. Additionally, they may engage in excessive chatting and generate a considerable amount of noise. Furthermore, these individuals may frequently transition from one object to another or exhibit a constant state of mobility.

Impulsivity is a psychological trait characterized by a tendency to act on immediate urges or desires

Impulsivity is an additional characteristic indicative of Attention-Deficit/Hyperactivity Disorder (ADHD). The subsequent manifestations denote indications of impulsive behavior in your child:

Exhibiting a severe lack of tolerance towards others

The act of disregarding one's turn in a game or activity when engaging with peers.

Disrupting interpersonal discourse

Engaging in the act of making inappropriate remarks

Individuals may encounter challenges in regulating their emotions.

Exhibiting a proclivity for emotional outbursts.

Engaging in uninvited participation during recreational activities without prior consent

Once more, these behaviors are frequently observed in young children between the ages of one and three, commonly referred to as toddlers. The concerns would only arise if they exhibited severe behaviors in relation to their peers of similar age. There are additional potential indicators of Attention-Deficit/Hyperactivity Disorder (ADHD) in children between the ages of

3 and 4 years. Children in this particular age group are susceptible to sustaining injuries as a result of excessive running or non-compliance with given directions. In addition to the core symptoms, individuals with ADHD may have supplementary manifestations such as aggressive conduct during play and a diminished sense of caution when interacting with unfamiliar individuals.

The manifestation of excessive bravado entails the act of placing oneself or others at risk due to an absence of fear. Furthermore, an inability to successfully execute the action of hopping on one foot is typically observed by the age of four.

As a parent, observing one's child experience a loss of self-regulation can provide a formidable challenge. Although it is not possible to eliminate anger entirely, it is within our capacity to educate our children on more effective strategies for managing it.

Identify stimuli that elicit a response.

It is important to be cognizant of the factors that contribute to the occurrence of furious outbursts in children. Is there a specific moment of the day when the occurrence of tantrums appears to reach its highest intensity? Is there anything that is particularly noteworthy or remarkable? Tantrums are anticipated to manifest within the specified periods:The post-school era is a significant challenge as it allows children to lower their defenses and express accumulated feelings.The instances in which individuals may experience hunger or fatigue are potential factors to consider.Certain stimuli or circumstances have the potential to elicit a strong reaction from your child, such as experiencing frustration when engaging in a particular task.

The implementation of early intervention measures is necessary.

As one's awareness of triggers increases, proactive intervention can be employed to prevent the manifestation of rage. Assume a comforting demeanor. If a youngster responds well to physical contact, it may be beneficial to gently stroke their back or arm. It is recommended to prompt individuals to engage in the act of counting to 10 while concurrently performing a deep inhalation and exhalation, as this practice has been shown to have potential benefits for mental and emotional well-being. Engage in this activity alongside them in order to facilitate their comprehension of this relaxation method.

It is advisable to engage in a period of rest and relaxation.

The implementation of time out as a disciplinary strategy does not necessarily need to be punitive in nature. Time out is a highly effective strategy for enabling a child to disengage from a potentially overwhelming circumstance and engage in a period of relaxation and respite. It is advisable to contemplate the option of temporarily disengaging from a situation in the following manner. Select an opportune moment during which your child exhibits a state of tranquility and contentment to engage in a conversation regarding the proper utilization of the time out technique. It is recommended to provide your child with the opportunity to select a designated time-out chair situated in a secluded area of the household, so affording them a sense of autonomy and control over the situation. Individuals will acquire the necessary knowledge and skills to effectively utilize the aforementioned tool at the appropriate time. Commend your child for effectively employing the time-out strategy to regulate their emotions, followed by engaging in a constructive dialogue to explore the circumstances behind the incident. In the event that a child's anger leads to the destruction and breakage of their crayons, it is advisable to inquire about alternative methods through which they could have effectively conveyed their emotions in a manner that is less detrimental and more constructive.

Classify the emotional states experienced by the individuals.

Take a moment to contemplate the emotional state of your child when you observe them experiencing frustration. The assembly of that puzzle presents a considerable challenge. It appears that the situation is eliciting a certain degree of frustration from you. By engaging in this practice, parents can facilitate the development of emotional self-awareness in their children. As the child's cognitive development progresses, parental support can be provided to facilitate the process of emotional identification and expression. In the event that the teacher informs you of your kid's challenging social interactions during the day, it is advisable to allocate time for a conversation with your child to discuss their emotional state. Facilitate effective communication of your child's emotions by encouraging them to articulate their feelings verbally.

Please present a range of alternatives.

Providing choices to one's youngster fosters a perception of empowerment. If one is aware that their child encounters difficulties during transitions, such as clean-up time, it is advisable to provide them an option as a means to facilitate their successful completion of the task. Which task would you want to commence with: tidying up the blocks or organizing the race cars? It is imperative to limit the number of possibilities to a maximum of two or three. An excessive number of possibilities might lead to feelings of overload or overstimulation in a child.

Conduct an assessment to see if your child is obtaining an adequate amount of sleep.

Sleep difficulties are frequently observed in children diagnosed with Attention Deficit Disorder (ADD) or Attention Deficit Hyperactivity Disorder (ADHD). Insufficient sleep in children is associated with heightened levels of irritability and moodiness. Individuals with attention deficit disorder (ADD) or attention deficit hyperactivity disorder (ADHD) exhibit heightened challenges in managing stress, displaying increased susceptibility to irritability, and experiencing a progressive exacerbation of their symptoms as the day progresses.

Exemplify proficient anger management skills through personal conduct.

Children diagnosed with Attention Deficit Disorder (ADD) or Attention Deficit Hyperactivity Disorder (ADHD) encounter difficulties in regulating their emotional responses.Enhancing a child's comprehension of their emotions and fostering their ability to recognize and choose alternate, more beneficial approaches of reacting might provide positive outcomes. One approach involves demonstrating a positive model. The pedagogical approach should prioritize the use of exemplification, when parents not only respond appropriately but also demonstrate the desired behavior to facilitate comprehension in their children.

Engage in collaborative reading activities

Please visit the library and choose books pertaining to emotions, with a particular focus on anger, resentment, rejection, loneliness, melancholy, or any other challenging feelings that your child frequently encounters. It is advisable to seek recommendations from the librarian. Engage in the activity of reading these narratives aloud to your child and thereafter engage in a discussion regarding the emotions evoked by the stories. Examine the manner in which the character manages their emotional states. What are the characters' responses or emotional responses to the situation? Is it possible that an other approach may have been employed in managing the situation? What would be your response if you found yourself in a comparable circumstance? Collectively, the characters collaborate to resolve issues and engage in deliberations over constructive measures they can undertake.

Engage in Meaningful Interactions

It is advisable to cultivate a routine of engaging in individualized interactions with one's child on a regular basis. Ensure that this period of interaction is characterized by a constructive, affectionate, and supportive atmosphere. Children diagnosed with Attention

Deficit Disorder (ADD) or Attention Deficit Hyperactivity Disorder (ADHD) sometimes encounter adverse experiences. It is imperative for individuals to comprehend the extent to which they are esteemed and cherished. As a parent, your influence has a significant role in shaping your child's positive self-esteem. The allocation of time in your presence is of utmost importance.

What are the methods for cultivating gratitude?

One effective method for cultivating this habit is through the use of a thankfulness diary. A thankfulness diary is a daily practice in which individuals record the things they are thankful for, as suggested by its name. When faced with a challenge, it is advisable to thoroughly explore the underlying reasons for expressing gratitude towards the existence of the challenge. For example, if your young child exhibits a tendency to remove their clothing in public, it is advisable to adopt a perspective of gratitude, recognizing the cognitive abilities of your child in successfully disrobing.

While acknowledging the importance of thankfulness, it is crucial to recognize that it does not possess inherent transformative powers. The cessation of anger does not occur instantaneously upon the commencement of gratitude. Over time, with consistent daily practice, the habit will become deeply ingrained within you, leading to a transformation in which you will experience gratitude towards the identical circumstances that previously elicited anger. In due course, the many components will converge harmoniously.

Please rephrase the user's text to be more formal and academic in tone. Lives characterized by excessive disarray and disorder

In our pursuit of enhanced productivity and the completion of numerous tasks, we frequently compromise our tranquility in favor of becoming adept practitioners of time management. The individual responds to electronic correspondence within the confines of a bathroom, formulates an impeccable sales presentation while waiting in a line, and completes all self-employed tasks while simultaneously engaging in recreational activities with their offspring in the outdoor area of their residence.

It is important to note that efficiency is highly valued. This is a characteristic that one would desire for their offspring to acquire from oneself. Nevertheless, the attempt to complete each individual task on your agenda is likely to result in feelings of being overwhelmed. In truth, stress and fury reciprocally amplify one another. In a momentary lapse, one may observe oneself succumbing to a surge of frustration upon witnessing a minor error committed by one's child, stemming from one's own inability to adhere to a personally established timeframe. The manifestation of your angry outburst was exacerbated by the pressure of meeting your deadline.

It is essential to remain authentic to our own selves, as it is an inherent truth that our young children will inevitably engage in behaviors that elicit feelings of anger within us. Due to their limited understanding of real-world dynamics, their behavior may appear entirely irrational from our perspective. In order to respond in a composed manner, it is imperative that we maintain a clear and unburdened mental state. This achievement can only be realized through the deliberate prioritization of singular tasks.

The concept entails declining requests or opportunities with a frequency that is comparable to accepting them. The preference lies in reducing the number of events on one's calendar rather than increasing the number of activities. Engaging in this activity will effectively address a vital component of the enigma at hand, namely, your list of tasks to be accomplished. Currently, there does not appear to be a recognized accolade specifically designated for the most productive parent globally, although it is possible that such an award exists unbeknownst to us. What are the potential benefits of relinquishing the pursuit of being the singular individual of significance? If such an award were to exist, it would likely be accompanied by the accolade for the most burdened parent.

It is imperative to maintain a demeanor of respect.

It is imperative to maintain a demeanor of respect at all times. If a someone is concerned about their ability to manage their anger and maintain a courteous demeanor, it is advisable to take a break in order to regain composure. It is advisable to seek a settlement to the matter after attaining a state of emotional equilibrium.

The emphasis should be placed on the subject matter or content, rather than on individuals involved.

It is important to direct one's attention towards the factors that elicited anger, rather than fixating on the individuals implicated. This will facilitate the process of articulating and elucidating one's anger when the occasion arises. Adhering to professional standards will assist in maintaining a professional demeanor.

Harness the potential energy that fury affords.

When experiencing anger, the sudden surge of adrenaline can induce feelings of empowerment, confidence, and competence. This will be particularly advantageous if one experiences discomfort in acknowledging or articulating their anger, since it allows for the utilization of the potent emotional energy that rage brings. It is important to exercise caution, as negative energy has the potential to foster impulsive or harmful actions.

Could you please provide me with an answer to my inquiry?

Which statements exemplify strategies for acknowledging anger in a manner that promotes the constructive utilization of this emotion?

The manner in which Terry consistently shifts responsibility onto others has elicited a strong emotional response of anger inside me.

The emotion that I have been misinterpreting as fear is, in fact, anger. It is imperative for me to address and overcome this emotional state in order to cease using my energy and potential on suppressing my wrath.

Coping with the persistent occurrences of system faults can be a source of frustration; nonetheless, it is imperative to cultivate the virtue of patience as a means of addressing this issue.

Kyle, will you kindly refrain from raising your voice at me? I am currently experiencing emotional distress, and I find it challenging to maintain focus in the presence of your raised voice.

The response to the user's query is as follows.

choice 1: This particular choice is deemed to be accurate. Recognizing and acknowledging one's anger inside is a crucial aspect of effectively harnessing anger for constructive purposes.

choice 2: This particular choice is deemed to be accurate. Frequently, individuals exhibit a lack of awareness in identifying anger, instead erroneously attributing it to alternative emotions or states. Recognizing and acknowledging one's anger is a crucial step towards effectively utilizing anger as a catalyst for achieving favorable outcomes within a professional setting.

choice 3: This particular choice is deemed to be wrong. Initially, it is imperative to recognize and acknowledge one's emotional state of anger. Engaging in rationalizations and attributing other labels to one's anger will not facilitate the constructive channeling of this emotion.

choice 4: This particular choice is deemed to be wrong. Experiencing verbal aggression from a colleague is likely to elicit feelings of anger in the majority of individuals. Recognizing and acknowledging anger can be a more effective approach since it presents the potential for facilitating constructive transformations.

It is important to acknowledge that the process of managing anger requires a significant amount of time. Anger is a complex emotion that accumulates and develops throughout an individual's lifespan. It is inherent that one should not anticipate an immediate cessation, nor should one anticipate an abrupt discontinuation. One should be willing to allocate a significant amount of time towards the process of improvement, experiment with various approaches to overcome obstacles, and acknowledge that occasional setbacks may occur, however maintaining a resilient mindset to persistently bounce back.

Document your improvement - Take both mental and written records of your current emotional state. Maintain a personal notebook wherein one diligently documents instances of anger, accompanying cognitive processes, and the duration of such affective states. As one continues to engage in anger management techniques, it is advisable to maintain a record of episodes characterized by intense anger. Even in the event of a marginal reduction in these factors, it can be inferred that progress is being made.

Identify the issues - On occasion, documenting one's progress can reveal a discernible pattern in the manifestation of one's anger. It is possible that individuals commonly experience heightened anger upon returning home following an extended period of work. In such instances, individuals may consider engaging in activities that promote relaxation or implementing strategies to reduce their burden. One may experience heightened frustration when encountering traffic congestion, prompting the consideration of other routes or adjustments to the timing of travel. Modifying one's schedule and seeking substitutes for sources of frustration can yield a more substantial impact on one's well-being than initially anticipated.

Value self-acknowledgment — Establish significant benchmarks for personal growth and experience a sense of accomplishment upon their attainment. It is advisable to adopt a proactive approach in interpersonal conflicts, particularly with one's spouse, by refraining from employing harmful language and instead expressing one's thoughts and concerns pertaining to the specific issue under discussion. Upon successfully doing this task, it is important to acknowledge and value one's efforts, so fostering a sense of self-appreciation. Additionally, it is advisable to establish a more ambitious objective for future endeavors. An further effective strategy for cultivating motivation involves engaging in discussions with a confidant regarding one's anger management journey, so sharing updates on personal growth and development. Expressing gratitude can have a significant impact on one's motivation and perseverance.

In the event of experiencing emotional distress due to a specific occurrence, it is recommended to employ the subsequent diary prompts as a means to articulate and contemplate upon this situation. This exercise can facilitate introspection and subsequent discussion with a trusted individual.

What specific occurrence took place?

Did the experience elicit feelings of anguish or stress, and if so, what were the underlying reasons for these emotional responses?

● What were your cognitive processes during such instances?

● Please indicate the level of anger you experienced during that particular moment on a scale ranging from 0 to 10.

What is your current level of anger on a scale of 0 to 10?

Did your behavior undergo any modifications as a consequence of experiencing anger?

Did the behavior of others undergo any modifications in response to your expression of anger?

● Prior to the occurrence, what were your emotional states? Were you previously experiencing feelings of tension, stress, irritation, and fatigue?

How did the individual's physiological system react to the given circumstances? Did the individual experience an increased heart rate, perspiration on the palms, or a headache?

● What was your intended course of action during that particular instance?

Did you successfully accomplish your intended objective, or did you engage in an alternative course of action?

- What are your current sentiments regarding the situation?

Were there any repercussions or outcomes that occurred as a result of the incident?

Assessing the Severity of Your Anger

It may be advantageous to assess the intensity of one's anger by employing a straightforward rating system. This approach facilitates the quantification of emotions and aids in the identification of suitable responses for various circumstances.

As an illustration, the grading scale employed by the author is as follows:

- A - I do not experience feelings of anger. ● B - I experience a sense of irritation, but it does not escalate to the level of anger. ● C - I am currently experiencing anger. ● D - I am currently experiencing anger, and I am unable to regulate or manage it. ● F - I am experiencing intense anger that significantly impairs my ability to operate properly and exhibit compassionate or adult behavior.

In the process of documenting my rage experiences, I consistently incorporate an evaluative metric denoted as the 'anger grade' at the commencement of each page. I find it beneficial to review my written work after attaining a state of emotional composure. Monitoring my "anger level" has shown to be quite advantageous in ensuring appropriate anger management, promptly identifying the onset of anger, and responding to anger in a constructive and adult manner.

Furthermore, it is imperative to prioritize making prudent decisions for one's own well-being, particularly when endeavoring to regulate one's anger. The presence of inadequate sleep, an unhealthy diet, and other unfavorable lifestyle choices can intensify feelings of rage and impede effective anger management.

www.ingramcontent.com/pod-product-compliance
Lightning Source LLC
Chambersburg PA
CBHW052141110526
44591CB00012B/1805